MW00908021

TRULY OBSCURE!

PRO FOOTBALL TRIVIA

Over 1,000 things you didn't know about the NFL, AFL, USFL, XFL, and AAFC...

Edited by: Tarrant Brothers

Introduction

Georgia is on the East Coast, and yet the Atlanta Falcons played in the NFC West for over thirty years. Ever wonder why? One current NFL franchise was once known as the Racine Normals. Curious as to which team it is? Those little star-like shapes on the Steelers' helmets are actually called a very specific term. Interested in what it might be? If so, you're the kind of fan for whom *TRULY OBSCURE NFL Trivia* was written.

One of the many elements which makes football the most compelling of all sports is, for lack of a better term, its many oddities. The bizarre plays. The colorful characters. The way a single bounce of a fumbled ball can make or break a team's entire season. Especially if you're a fan of trivia, the history of the sport is a goldmine of strange facts and crazy coincidences.

Assuming you've been following the sport for a while, you're going to be familiar with a good amount of football trivia already. You've probably heard of the "Heidi Game". The first thing that comes to mind when you hear the name Jim Marshall is not that he was one of the most durable players in history (starting a then-record 270 consecutive games), but rather that he's the guy who picked up a fumble and ran it 60 yards in the wrong direction. And there's no telling how many times you've heard that the Super Bowl got its name from some kid's toy.

Even if you are familiar with the most well-known bits of NFL trivia, this book will expose you to factoids you've never come across before. The TRULY OBSCURE team has scoured the football universe to uncover the strangest, wackiest, and, well, most obscure facts that relate to the great game of professional football. We traveled back to the NFL's humble beginnings in the 1920s, and also mined trivia from the various rival leagues that sprung up over the years. If you're a longtime hardcore fan of the game, you may have heard a handful of these, but we're guessing no more than that.

So sit back, relax, grab a cold one and prepare to become *the* biggest know-it-all at your next tailgate party.

A Guide to the Other American Football Leagues

While the NFL has long been the major league of professional football in America, it has not been without its occasional competitor. Since this book covers trivia from all professional leagues, here is a quick guide to upstart leagues which took on the NFL, with varying degrees of success and longevity.

The All-American Football Conference (AAFC) 1946-1949

The AAFC was formed as the first serious competitor to the established NFL in 1944, the brainchild of Chicago Tribune sports editor Arch Ward. Ward, who had previously originated All-Star Games for both Major League Baseball and college football, brought together a number of wealthy football enthusiasts, some of whom had been unable to secure NFL franchises. By 1946, the AAFC began play with eight teams in two divisions representing New York, Brooklyn, Buffalo, Miami, Cleveland, Chicago, Los Angeles, and San Francisco. The Cleveland franchise, having made the bold move of hiring Paul Brown as their coach, was the dominant team in the AAFC, winning all four league championships and posting a record of 54-4-3.

While the AAFC experienced some success, on occasion drawing crowds as large as 83,000 for big games, the league as a whole was losing money and franchises were being forced to fold. By

1949, only seven teams were still in business and the league was in danger of going under. However, the NFL agreed to a merger and accepted the Browns, San Francisco 49ers, and Baltimore Colts into their league, assuring that the legacy of the AAFC would continue. (This was a different Colts franchise than the one that would later move to Indianapolis.)

The American Football League (AFL) 1960-1970

As pro football gained popularity, more and more businessmen became interested in owning NFL franchises. The AFL was created by a group of men who had been refused NFL expansion franchises or had minor shares of NFL franchises. The AFL's original lineup saw an Eastern division of the New York Titans (later the Jets), Boston Patriots, Buffalo Bills and the Houston Oilers along with a Western division of the Los Angeles Chargers, Denver Broncos, Oakland Raiders, and Dallas Texans (now known as the Kansas City Chiefs). Later, the AFL would add the Cincinnati Bengals and Miami Dolphins.

The AFL struggled at first, but eventually gained a following as TV viewers began to enjoy the league's more colorful, offense-oriented style. The new league continued to offer large contracts to top college stars, leading to bidding wars and skyrocketing player salaries across the board. This eventually led to an agreement in 1966 for the two leagues to merge.

The leagues operated independently for the next four seasons, although they instituted a common draft and a championship game that soon became known as the Super Bowl. The NFL champion Green Bay Packers won the first two title games over the Kansas City Chiefs and Oakland Raiders. In Super Bowl III, however, the New York Jets pulled one of the great upsets in football history by defeating the Baltimore Colts, establishing the AFL as an equal to the older league.

After the 1970 season, the ten AFL franchises joined the NFL to form the American Football Conference along with the NFL's Pittsburgh Steelers, Cleveland Browns, and Baltimore Colts.

The World Football League (WFL) 1974-1975

Gary L. Davidson, founder of the successful American Basketball Association and World Hockey Association, believed he could start a football league to take on the NFL. While the WFL flamed out after only two seasons, it did cause waves by signing several key NFL players to contracts above what the elder league was paying. The WFL also tried to differentiate itself by playing a 20 game schedule and forgoing the traditional PAT with an "Action Point" play from scrimmage after a touchdown.

United States Football League (USFL) 1983-1985

The USFL was a spring/summer league which was founded by David Dixon, an antiques dealer who helped found the New Orleans Saints. Dixon spent years studying the AFL and WFL and eventually concluded that the market existed for a league to play during the NFL's off-season. Dixon's plan for the USFL centered around television revenue (the league signed deals with ABC and ESPN) and exposure in major markets (of the 12 original USFL teams, nine played in markets that had an NFL team as well). The league made headlines before play even began when the New Jersey Generals (owned by Donald Trump) signed University of Georgia star Hershel Walker to a contract despite Walker only being a junior in college.

On the field, the Philadelphia Stars (who moved to Baltimore for the 1985 season) were the league's most successful team, playing in all three league championship games and winning two of them. They were led by future NFL coach Jim Mora and featured several well-known players such as LB Sam Mills, RB Kelvin Bryant, and QB Chuck Fusina. The Stars were 48-13-1 overall.

Like most startup leagues, the USFL experienced financial issues and attendance woes that led to a number of teams relocating or folding outright. However, the league did manage three seasons of play before the decision was made (primarily at the urging of Trump) to move to a fall schedule in 1986 and compete with the NFL directly. Trump's thinking was that eventually the USFL and NFL would merge and USFL owners would see their teams double in value. However, many franchises were weary of competing with NFL teams in their cities and either moved, folded, or merged with other teams. By the time the USFL was ready to take on a fall schedule, only eight franchises remained.

Perhaps the USFL is most famous for its antitrust lawsuit against the NFL, in which the established league was accused of running a monopoly with regards to television rights and stadium access. The USFL asked for damages of $567 million and wanted to see the NFL split into two competing leagues or be forced to appear only on two television networks. A jury found in favor of the USFL, however, the league was only awarded one dollar as it was also found that its financial troubles were due to its own mismanagement and not malfeasance by the NFL.

The USFL ceased operation soon thereafter, never playing a fall schedule. A number of USFL players joined NFL teams and became stars, most notably Steve Young (of the LA Express), Reggie White (Memphis Showboats), Anthony Carter (Michigan Panthers), Jim Kelly (Houston Gamblers), in addition to the abovementioned Walker, Mills, and Bryant.

World League of American Football (WLAF) (1990-1992)

The WLAF was founded by the NFL in 1990 to serve as a developmental league and as a way to introduce American football to Europe. Games were played in the spring and featured teams in London, Frankfurt, and Barcelona along with American teams in mostly non-NFL cities such as Sacramento and Birmingham. The league lost money and ceased operations after two seasons.

NFL Europe (1995-2007)

The NFL resurrected the WLAF concept as a spring league consisting strictly of European teams, with play beginning in 1995. The three European teams from the WLAF were part of the original NFL Europe lineup, along with new teams in Amsterdam, Düsseldorf (who competed as Rhein Fire), and Edinburgh (known as the Scottish Claymores). The league experienced some success, mostly in Germany, but lost money each year and was shut down by the NFL after the 2007 season. A number of NFL quarterbacks gained experience early in their career in NFL Europe, most famously Kurt Warner, Brad Johnson, and Jake Delhomme, all of whom eventually led NFL teams to the Super Bowl. Jon Kitna, Scott Mitchell, Damon Huard and Jay Fielder also had solid careers as starters in the NFL after playing in Europe.

XFL (2001)

The XFL was created as a joint venture between the NBC television network and Vince McMahon of the World Wrestling Federation as a spring league that was not meant to compete with the NFL. Instead, it was designed to combine "real" football with the theatrics and over-the-top aggressiveness of professional wrestling. The rules were relaxed to promote a rougher game and players and coaches wore microphones during games and were encouraged to be confrontational towards one another. The XFL featured eight teams, mostly in non-NFL cities such as Memphis, Los Angeles, and Birmingham and gave them unusual, violent-sounding nicknames such as the Enforcers, Hitmen, and Maniax. While the XFL commanded a lot of media attention, the league quickly turned into a joke as fans quickly tuned out due to low-quality play, desperate attention-seeking stunts, and a general lack of respect from the sports media. NBC and the WWF each lost a reported $35 million and pulled the plug after one season. Only a handful of players made it to the NFL, most notably the XFL's MVP Tommy Maddox, who went on to win a Super Bowl with the Pittsburgh Steelers.

CHAPTER I: TAILGATE

NO PENALTY KICKS, HOWEVER: The last scoreless tie in the NFL was between the Detriot Lions and New York Giants in 1943.

WAR IS HELL – ON NICKNAMES: Due to so many players being enlisted during World War II, the Pittsburgh Steelers and Philadelphia Eagles combined to form the "Steagles" in 1943. They went 5-4-1.

TAKING MATTERS INTO YOUR OWN HANDS: Brad Johnson of the Vikings threw a touchdown pass to himself in 1997.

NOBODY'S PERFECT: In 1998, Gary Johnson of the Vikings became the first kicker in NFL history to make every FG and PAT attempt during an entire season. He then missed a late FG in the NFC championship game that would probably have clinched a Super Bowl berth.

WILLIE OR WON'T HE: The first African-American quarterback debuted for the Chicago Bears in 1943. His name, appropriately enough, was Willie Thrower.

DOMED FROM THE BEGINNING: Offensive lineman Bob Kowalkowski played in the first game in the Pontiac Silverdome in 1975. His son, linebacker Scott Kowalkowksi, played the Silverdome's final game in 2002. Both were members of the Lions.

HEY, AT LEAST IT WASN'T THE SENORITAS: The Oakland Raiders were originally to be nicknamed the Senors.

BOOKENDS: Record-breaking running back Emmitt Smith had 937 rushing yards during his first NFL season (1990, with the Cowboys). He also gained 937 yards during his last season (2004, with the Cardinals).

THE YOUNG AND THE LEFTIST: Steve Young, in 2005, became the first left-handed quarterback to be enshrined in the Pro Football Hall of Fame.

SKIN IN THE GAME: It takes about 3,000 cows to supply a year's worth of leather for NFL footballs.

'CANE MUTINY: Six members of the University of Miami Hurricanes were selected in the first round of the 2004 NFL draft, a record for a single school. They were: Sean Taylor (#5 pick, Redskins), Kellen Winslow, Jr. (#6, Browns), Jonathan Vilma (#12, Jets), D.J. Williams (#17, Broncos), Vernon Carey (#19, Dolphins), and Vince Wilfork (#21, Patriots).

THE LAST WILL BE FIRST: 1993 featured the only eight round draft in NFL history, yet six future Pro Bowl players were picked in that final round. (QB Trent Green, QB Elvis Grbac, WR Troy Brown, LB Jessie Armstead, S Blaine Bishop and P Craig Hentrich)

GUYS, THIS IS STARTING TO GET OLD: John Elway was sacked 516 times in his career, a record.

STICK TO BASEBALL, FELLAS: In 1934, the Brooklyn Dodgers only scored one rushing touchdown all season. They still managed to go 4-7 on the year.

DAY OFF FOR THE LITTLE GUYS: On September 13, 1992, the Bills and the 49ers played an entire game without a single punt. The Bills won 34-21 thanks to Jim Kelly's 403 yards passing and

3 touchdowns. The teams combined for 1086 yards of total offense.

TECHNICALLY, THERE'S ALSO LOSING AND TYING: College football coach Red Sanders coined the expression "Winning isn't everything, it's the only thing" in Sports Illustrated several years before Vince Lombardi more famously said it.

SOMEBODY IN MARKETING EARNED HIS PAYCHECK: Super Bowl III was actually the first game to be called "the Super Bowl". Super Bowls I and II were named as such retroactively. At the time each was called the "AFL-NFL Championship Game".

BULLISH ON THE DOGS: The longest NFL unbeaten streak is held by the Canton Bulldogs, who went 22-0-3 during the 1922-23 seasons.

GOOD EVERY TEN YEARS: The Packers and the Giants are the only franchises to win Super Bowls in three different decades.

ONLY WIMPS TAKE PLAYS OFF: Chuck Bednarik of the Eagles was the last NFL player to play significant minutes on both sides of the ball, doing so in 1960 as a center on offense and linebacker on defense.

AND YES, WE WILL COUNT THEM: Each NFL home team is required to provide 24 footballs for each game.

MONEY DOESN'T GROWN ON TREES, YA KNOW: There have been six total work stoppages (strikes/lockouts) in NFL history.

A REALLY SHORT BOX SCORE: If an NFL team forfeits a game, the score will be recorded as 2-0 as a safety is the only score that is not accredited to a single player.

HAVE YOU SEEN HOWARD'S LUNCH? On November 23, 1970, announcer Howard Cosell got drunk and vomited on Don Meredith's boots during a broadcast of ABC's Monday Night Football.

SURPRISED IT'S NOT 99 PERCENT? 80% of Super Bowl tickets go to corporate sponsors.

RELIEF PITCHER: In 1994, NFL quarterback Peyton Manning was a backup at the University of Tennessee. He got to chance to play due to an injury to starter Todd Helton, who became one of the best pitchers in baseball with the Colorado Rockies.

DON'T ASK US WHY: If the snap goes between the quarterback's legs, the ball is ruled dead if the quarterback does not pick it up. If another player picks it up, a false start penalty is given to the offense. It is not a fumble that can be returned by the defense.

NOW IF THEY COULD ACTUALLY WIN ONE: The Arizona Cardinals appeared in the Super Bowl in 2009. This ended a dry spell of championship game appearances that stretched back to 1947 when the team was in Chicago.

IF THAT'S THE WAY IT'S GONNA BE, I'LL START MY OWN TEAM: When Babe Ruth joined the New York Yankees, the player he replaced in right field was future Chicago Bears founder George Halas.

A GUY CAN'T ACCEPT EVERY JOB OFFER: Olympic gold medalist sprinter Carl Lewis was selected by the Dallas Cowboys in the 12th round of the 1984 draft as a wide receiver. He was also selected that year by the Chicago Bulls of the NBA. Lewis never played for either team.

A SIGN OF THINGS TO COME (MAYBE): The first play in team history for both the New Orleans Saints and Miami Dolphins were opening kickoffs returned for touchdowns.

I DON'T THINK "CASTRATED" IS THE IMAGE WE WANT TO PROJECT: The Dallas Cowboys were originally to be named the Steers.

GET THE PAIN OUT OF THE WAY FIRST: On Sept 24th 1950 Jim Hardy of the Chicago Cardinals threw an NFL record eight interceptions in a game. The next week, he turned things around by throwing six touchdowns, one shy of the league record.

NEON LIGHTS 'EM UP: In 1989, cornerback Deion Sanders became the only person to hit an MLB home run and score an NFL touchdown in the same week.

BECAUSE ONLY A KICKER WOULD THINK THIS UP: The Nerf football was invented by former Vikings kicker Fred Cox in 1972.

RAIN AND SNOW? NO PROBLEM: All NFL stadiums are required to be built facing north/south so the sun never interferes with a play.

HEY, THIS IS EASY: In 1995 the Carolina Panthers were the first expansion team to defeat the defending Super Bowl champion when they knocked off the San Francisco 49ers.

A REAL PARDEE ANIMAL: Jack Pardee is the only man to serve as a head coach in the NFL, USFL, CFL, WFL, and NCAA.

FROM THE MAILROOM TO THE CORNER OFFICE: Dick Vermeil was the NFL's first ever special teams coach, hired by the Rams in 1969. Thirty-one years later, he coached the Rams to their first NFL title.

WE DON'T CARE, JUST GET US OUT OF LA-LA LAND: The Los Angeles Rams almost moved to Baltimore before relocating to St. Louis in 2005.

A TRIPLE BRETT: Quarterback Brett Favre is the only person who has ever won the NFL's MVP award in three consecutive seasons.

MOON OVER CANTON: Former Oilers quarterback Warren Moon is the only undrafted quarterback in the NFL Hall of Fame.

YES, THIS IS A REAL THING IN TEXAS: Running back Earl Campbell of the Houston Oilers is an Official State Hero of Texas, joining Davy Crockett, Sam Houston, and Stephen F. Austin.

AND YOU CALL HIM A BUM: Houston Oilers Coach Bum Phillips was known for wearing a cowboy hat while on the sidelines; however, he never wore it in domed stadiums. Phillips claimed that "My mama told me never to wear a hat indoors."

FROM CHUMP TO CHAMP: The first player ever cut by the expansion Carolina Panthers in 1995 was defensive tackle Bill Goldberg, who later became a professional wrestling superstar.

HARD TO BELIEVE "THE NORMALS" NEVER CAUGHT ON: The franchise currently known as the Arizona Cardinals has also been known as the Morgan Athletic Club, the Racine Normals, the Racine Cardinals, the Chicago Cardinals, the St. Louis Cardinals, the Phoenix Cardinals, and finally the Arizona Cardinals. Despite the many name changes, the team is the oldest continuous franchise in football history.

IT'S A BASEBALL TOWN, ANYWAY: The Cardinals were in St. Louis for 28 years and did not host a single postseason game; they made the playoffs three times, each time playing only road games.

COMING FULL CIRCLE: Offensive lineman Dan Dierdorf and defensive lineman Alan Page are the only two players in the Hall of Fame who were raised in Canton,Ohio.

NEVER COUNT OUT STEVE DEBERG: In 1996, after coming out of retirement to play for the Falcons at the age of 44, backup quarterback Steve DeBerg became the oldest player to appear on the roster of a Super Bowl team.

THEY SHOULD HAVE GIVEN HIM ONE MORE CHANCE: During the only season Green Bay Packer great Brett Favre played for the Atlanta Falcons, he threw for zero completions on four attempts. Two of those attempts were interceptions.

SO INSTEAD THEY WENT WITH HECKYL AND JECKYL: The Ravens changed team logos after their third season due to a lawsuit by a security guard who had designed the logo and faxed it to the team headquarters but had never received credit or payment for his design.

RUNNING INTO A WALL: In 51 consecutive games stretching from 1998 to 2001, the Baltimore Ravens defense did not allow any running back to gain over 100 yards.

YES, THAT SCOTT NORWOOD: During the time of the USFL, the Birmingham Stallions had on their roster at the same time former Bills Running Back Joe Cribbs and future Bills Kicker Scott Norwood.

TECHNICALLY, IT WAS STILL PRO FOOTBALL: Former Bills offensive guard Billy Shaw is the only member of the Pro Football Hall of Fame to have never played in the NFL (his entire career was spent in the AFL).

AND YOU THOUGHT HE WAS JUST A PRETTY FACE: Former NFL Coach and TV commentator John Madden was drafted by the Eagles in 1958. He was injured in training camp and never played in a regular season game.

THEN THEY THOUGHT, MAYBE WE SHOULD TRY LIGHTS INSTEAD: In the early 1950s, the NFL used a white ball with brown stripes for night games.

CHAPTER II: COIN TOSS

NOT JUST YOUR AVERAGE CYCLOIDS: The three shapes on the Steeler's logo are known as hypocycloids and represent the three elements that make up steel (iron, carbon, and sulfur).

FIRST, THEY HAD TO MOVE THE LIVING ROOM FURNITURE: The first indoor NFL game was played in Chicago in 1932 on a modified 80 yard field, due to harsh winter weather.

COLOR US SURPRISED: The last NFL team to integrate an African-American player onto the squad was the Washington Redskins, who signed WR Billy Mitchell in 1962.

YEAH, BUT HOW WAS HIS JUMP SHOT? Only one man has been inducted into the Hall of Fame for both the pro football and pro baseball: Cal Hubbard, an offensive lineman for the Giants and Packers in the 20's and 30's and later a major league umpire.

KIND OF DEFEATS THE PURPOSE: The first NFL team on the west coast was the Los Angeles Buccaneers, who in 1926 played all their games on the road.

SURE, I WAS LOOKING FOR A SECOND JOB ANYWAY: Johnny Unitas was working as a pile driver operator in Pittsburgh when the Baltimore Colts called him in for a tryout.

DON'T ASK ABOUT VERSIONS 1 – 4: The NFL's first successful facemask was known as the "B5" ("bar tubular, fifth version") developed by the Riddell sporting goods with the help of Paul

Brown, who wanted to protect quarterback Otto Graham's broken jaw.

BEFORE I GIVE YOU THE NEXT PLAY, A WORD FROM OUR SPONSORS: The first use of an in-helmet radio was in 1956 by Browns quarterback George Ratterman. It was developed by head coach Paul Brown as a means to call in plays. It was banned by the NFL after a few games and the in-helmet radio did not return until 1994.

CENTURY? DON'T ASK: The NFL first aligned into divisions in 1967. The four divisions were named the Capital, Century, Central, and Coastal.

AND YOU THINK THE LEAGUE WILL DO ANYTHING FOR MONEY NOW: From 1960 to 1969, the NFL staged a game in Miami called the Playoff Bowl between the runner-ups in each division to determine the league's third-place winner.

THE SHAPE(S) OF THINGS TO COME: The first ever NFL game was in 1920 and featured the Columbus Panhandles against the Dayton Triangles. The Panhandles folded after 1926.

BUT THEY COULDN'T COMPETE WITH BIG-MARKET GREEN BAY: The smallest town to ever host an NFL franchise was LaRue, Ohio. It was home in 1922 and 1923 to the Oorang Indians.

FROM CHAMPS TO CHUMPS: The 1928 NFL champions were the Providence Steamrollers. The Steamrollers were the last team that is not currently part of the NFL to win a title. They folded after the 1931 season.

PAY ATTENTION, THIS WILL BE ON THE QUIZ: The Baltimore Colts folded in 1950 after a single season. In 1953, a new

Baltimore Colts began play and are currently known as the Indianapolis Colts.

ONE OF THESE THREE IS NOT LIKE THE OTHER: In 1922, Chicago was home to three teams: the Cardinals, the Bears, and the Racine Maroons.

IT WAS EITHER THAT OR THE DARK PINKS: The Cardinals got their name in 1901 because the team wore used jerseys from the University of Chicago, which were originally maroon but had faded to a cardinal red color.

LONG BEFORE MANNING VS. BRADY: The first AFL game was on September 9, 1960, between the Denver Broncos and the Boston Patriots.

MAYBE WE SHOULD CONSIDER PLANNING THIS A LITTLE BETTER: In the beginning years of the NFL, there was no set schedule. Teams played as many as 15 games and as few as four. It wasn't until 1933 that the league had a standard schedule and two divisions that led to a championship game.

A MAN WITH PRIORITIES: Former Saints and Redskins running back George Rogers once said, "I want to rush for 1,000 or 1,500 yards, whichever comes first."

ANY SANDLOT MAIMINGS ARE PURELY INCIDIENTAL: Former Bears linebacker Dick Butkus once said, "I wouldn't ever set out to hurt anyone deliberately unless it was important -- like a league game".

IT'S HARD TO BE BOTH MODEST *AND* HONEST: Former 49ers and Raiders wide receiver Jerry Rice once said, "I feel like I'm the best, but you're not going to get me to say that."

GOOD THING THIS WAS BEFORE "PAPER OR PLASTIC?" The tradition of fans of losing teams wearing bags over their heads was started in New Orleans in 1980. The Saints went 1-15 that season and a group of fans started the "Bag Heads."

BABY STEPS: It took the Saints 21 seasons to finally finish one with a winning record. They promptly lost their first playoff game to the Vikings.

ONE OUT OF FOUR AIN'T BAD: The Saints were originally in the Capital Division in 1967 along with the Redskins, Cowboys, and Eagles.

PLUS, THEY WON THE SUPER BOWL: The 1979 Steelers were the first team in history whose roster was comprised entirely of players drafted by the Steelers or signed as undrafted free agents. Nobody on the team had ever played for any other NFL franchise.

IF IT HAD BEEN A BAD DAY, HE WOULD HAVE BOUGHT THE CARDINALS: Legend has it that Art Rooney, Sr. paid the initial franchise fee to start the Steelers with his winnings after a good day at the race track.

LAST STOP FOR THOSE 3,000 COWS: All NFL footballs are made in Ada, Ohio, by the Wilson company.

ANY DON'T TRY TO USE ANY OF LAST YEAR'S: Each NFL team is annually shipped 108 footballs – 54 for games and 54 for practices.

A MYSTERY RIGHT UP THERE WITH HOFFA AND JFK: It is unknown exactly who designed the Cowboy's "star" logo.

NICE PUTT...NOW CLEAN OUT YOUR OFFICE: In February of 1989, Dallas Cowboys new owner Jerry Jones informed head coach Tom Landry that he was fired just as Landry had finished a round of golf.

SO FAR, JERRY JONES HAS NOT YET SUED OVER THIS: Tom Landry's gravestone in the Texas State Cemetery in Austin features both the Cowboy's star logo and a depiction of Landry's trademark fedora.

YOU LIKE ME. YOU REALLY LIKE ME: Former Eagles and Rams coach Dick Vermeil was named national coach of the year at four different levels: high school, junior college, NCAA Division I, and NFL.

FANS IN HIGH PLACES: In 1979, Eagles quarterbacks Ron Jaworski and Joe Pisarcik (both of Polish heritage) received medals from Pope John Paul II during a visit to Philadelphia.

DITKA? HE'LL NEVER AMOUNT TO ANYTHING: Future Hall of Fame executive Jim Finks resigned from the Bears in 1982 after owner George Halas hired Mike Ditka as head coach without consulting him.

YOU CAN'T REALLY HURT PEOPLE AS COACH: Former Bears linebacker Dick Butkus was originally to be the Head Coach of the Chicago Enforcers of the XFL. He resigned to take another position within the league.

OUR NEXT ORDER OF BUSINESS...HOW TO DEFEND AGAINST THE RUN-AND-SHOOT: Former Bengals LB and Dartmouth graduate Reggie Williams served on the Cincinnati City Council while a member of the team.

COACH BROWN, WE LOVE YA BUT WE CAN'T TURN DOWN NAMING RIGHTS FOREVER: For a few years, Paul Brown had two NFL stadiums named after him: Paul Brown Stadium in Cincinnati and Cleveland Browns stadium a few miles away.

IT'S GOOD TO BE AN INSIDER: Paul Brown only went through with his plan to form the Bengals in the AFL because he was assured that an AFL-NFL merger was forthcoming.

WE WON'T COUNT THE GAMES IN TORONTO: Of the original eight AFL teams, only the Broncos and Bills have never moved from their original cities.

SPORTS AND POLITICS DON'T (REALLY) MIX: Broncos wide receiver Rick Upchurch was briefly engaged to future Secretary of State Condoleezza Rice in the 1970s.

LET'S SEE...CRAIG MORTON...AND...UH: Before John Elway joined the Broncos in 1983 the team had gone through 24 starting quarterbacks in its 21 year history.

HARD TO BELIEVE THOSE DIDN'T GO OVER WELL: The Bronco's original brown-and-mustard uniforms were so hated that a public bonfire was conducted to burn the infamous vertically striped socks after the team colors were changed.

THEY MADE UP FOR IT BY NOT WINNING MUCH AT HOME, EITHER: The Detroit Lions are the only team to go three consecutive seasons (2001-2003) without a victory on the road.

NOT MUCH EVER GOES RIGHT FOR DETROIT: Lions wide receiver Chuck Hughes died of a heart attack during a game in 1971. The team retired his #85 jersey.

ALSO KNOWN AS "THE TRIPLETS": The Lions have had three head coaches named "Clark": George Clark (1931-36, 1940), Earl Clark (1937-38) and Monte Clark (1978-1984).

BUT HOW WILL PEOPLE KNOW WHAT STATE WE'RE IN? The current edition of the Houston Texans is actually the sixth pro football team to use that nickname. The original Dallas Texan folded in 1952. A later edition of the Dallas Texans moved to Kansas City and became the Chiefs. A World Football League version of the Houston Texans moved to Shreveport, Louisiana. An Arena Football league version of the Dallas Texans played a few seasons in the 1990s. Finally, the Sacramento Gold Miners of the Canadian Football League moved to San Antonio and played as the Texans for one season before folding.

BLACK HIGHTOPS OPTIONAL: The Colts' quarterback legend Johnny Unitas had a cameo as a football coach in Oliver Stone's 1999 film *Any Given Sunday*.

REMEMBER THE TITANS: The 1999 Jacksonville Jaguars finished their season 15-3 (counting playoff games). All three losses were to the Tennessee Titans.

YES, THIS PLACE REALLY EXISTS: The first NFL mascot introduced into the Mascot Hall of Fame (located in Newark, Deleware) was the Chief's K.C. Wolf in 2006.

WHAT ELSE ARE THEY GOING TO DUMP ON THE COACH? The Chiefs were the first team in the NFL to use Gatorade on the sidelines during games.

NUMBERS GAME: When quarterback Joe Montana was traded from the 49ers to the Chiefs, he could not wear his signature #16 as it was retired by Kansas City in honor of former quarterback Len Dawson. Dawson offered to let Montana wear #16 anyway but Montana declined and wore #19 as a Chief.

A HEROIC NUMBER: Though not officially retired, no Chief has worn the #37 jersey since the death of running back Joe Delaney. (Delaney died in 1983 while attempting to save three drowning children. One survived.)

COMEBACK KID: In 2006, quarterback Chad Pennington of the Jets won the Comeback Player of the Year Award. Two seasons later, he won the same award as a member of the Dolphins.

IT JUST LOOKED LIKE THE KIND OF PLACE A QUARTERBACK WOULD BUILD: In the 1999 film *Any Given Sunday*, the set used as the house of Miami Sharks quarterback Cap Rooney (Dennis Quaid) was the actual house of Miami Dolphins great Dan Marino.

THE NFL WAS A LITTLE QUEASY ABOUT THE "EYEBALL" SCENE: Oliver Stone was unable to get permission to use NFL logos and team names in *Any Given Sunday*. So instead the fictional Associated Football Franchises of America league was created. However, the NFL still exists in the film as references are made to the Miami Dolphins' influence as to why the Sharks can't get a new stadium.

FINALLY, I CAN HANG 'EM UP: Quarterback Dan Marino only won one road playoff game in his entire Hall of Fame career, in 2000 against the Seahawks. It was also the last win of his career.

SERIOUSLY, THE LIONS GET NO RESPECT: The first ever Monday Night Football game at Detroit's Ford Field did not feature the Lions. (It was the Vikings versus Giants in 2010; the game was moved from Minnesota due to damage to the Metrodome's roof.)

GENTLEMEN, WE HAVE A BETTER SHOT AT LOSING SUPER BOWLS IN THE OTHER LEAGUE: The Minnesota Vikings were almost an AFL team. The ownership group originally applied to the AFL in 1961 but withdrew the application and joined the NFL instead.

WELL, THAT WAS KIND OF A WASTE: The 1998 Vikings were the first team to go 15-1 during the regular season and not make the Super Bowl.

HEY, I COULD DO THIS: Patriots QB Tom Brady was a big 49ers fan growing up and was actually in attendance at the famous 1981 "catch" playoff game versus the Cowboys.

BECAUSE IT SOUNDS LIKE A DIVISION III COLLEGE TEAM, PERHAPS? For a short time in 1971 the former Boston Patriots were known as the Bay State Patriots before finally settling on New England Patriots.

BABY STEPS, PART II: The New Orleans Saints were founded in 1967. They didn't win a playoff game until 2000.

A "SLICK" LOOKING UNIFORM: The Saints' team colors (black and gold) represent the city's long ties to the oil ("black gold") industry.

I THOUGHT *YOU* HAD CALLED THE COMMISH: In 1969, the Saints attempted to switch to a black helmet with a gold logo. They used them during the preseason but because they had not previously cleared the change with the league they were not allowed to be used in regular season games.

NOW THAT YOU MENTION IT, "BUM" IS NOT SO BAD: Former Houston Oilers and New Orleans Saints' coach Bum Philips' real first name was Oail.

JUST IN CASE THEY MOVE BACK: Even though the baseball Giants moved to San Francisco in 1957, the football team's corporate name remains The New York Football Giants, Inc.

WITH ASSISSTANTS LIKE THESE, WHO NEEDS A HEAD COACH? The 1956 Giants featured future Hall of Fame coach Vince Lombardi as offensive coordinator and future Hall of Fame coach Tom Landry as defensive coordinator.

IT'S GOOD TO HAVE A SOLID BACKUP PLAN: At the 1979 NFL draft, the San Francisco 49ers originally intended to draft Phil Simms. Because the Giants picked Simms first, the Niners had to go with their second choice: Joe Montana.

BUT THAT ONE BAD PASS, IT WAS A DOOZY: Perhaps the most underrated performance in a Super Bowl was that of Phil Simms against the Broncos in XXI. Simms completed 22 of 25 passes, and two of those incompletions were drops.

THE FRENCH CONNECTION: Three players with the first name Napoleon have played for the Raiders (McCallum, Kaufmann, and Harris).

THIS IS HOW YOU GET YOUR NAME ON A VIDEO GAME: In ten years as coach of the Oakland Raiders, John Madden's teams finished first in their division seven times and second the other three.

AL DAVIS: CIVIL RIGHTS HERO? The Raiders were the first team to hire a Hispanic head coach (Tom Flores) and the first to hire an African-American head coach (Art Shell).

A JOINER WAS THE FINAL QUITTER: Chargers wide receiver Charlie Joiner was the last active AFL player to play in the NFL. He retired in 1987.

ONLY BECAUSE ANDRE THE GIANT NEVER PLAYED: The largest (measured) hands of any player in NFL history belonged to 49ers wide receiver John Taylor.

AT LEAST THEY CAN'T HIT HIM UP FOR DONATIONS: Longtime journeyman quarterback Dave Krieg's alma mater, Milton College, no longer exists.

BIGGER FISH TO FRY: The Cleveland Rams sat out the 1943 NFL season due to player shortages caused by World War II.

SPIES LIKE THEM: One of the companies purchased by Tampa Bay Buccaneers owner Malcolm Glazer was a nearly bankrupt energy company called Zapata Oil. Zapata Oil was originally founded by future CIA chief and President of the United States George H.W. Bush. Some claim that Zapata Oil was once a front of the CIA.

NO WONDER THEY COULDN'T WIN A GAME: The Tampa Bay Buccaneers, during their first season in 1976, were part of the AFC West division.

THE CREAMSICLE JERSEYS WOULD HAVE STAYED, PRESUMABLY: Baltimore Orioles owner Peter Angelos attempted in 1994 to buy the Tampa Bay Buccaneers with the intention of moving them to Baltimore.

MULTI-STATE PRESENCE: The Washington Redskins are headquartered in Virginia and play their home games in Maryland.

IT KEPT HIM FROM BEING BLIND-SIDED: During the 1960s, Redskins running back Larry Brown had a hearing aid installed inside his helmet as he was nearly deaf.

CHAPTER III: KICKOFF

UNITY EQUALS STRENGTH: During the strike of 1987, the Redskins were the only team to not have any players cross the picket line to play with the replacement players. Washington went on to win the Super Bowl that season.

YOU MAY HAVE HEARD OF HIM: Longtime New York Jets coach Weeb Ewbank coached a young quarterback named Joe Paterno while at Brown University during the 1940's.

NEVER HURTS TO TRY: The Birmingham Americans and Memphis Southmen of the World Football League both attempted to join the NFL but were denied.

REALLY? I LIKE YOUR GUYS, TOO: After the inaugural USFL season in 1983, the owners of the Arizona Wranglers and Chicago Blitz traded their complete rosters to each other.

SURE, WE'LL CALL IT A DYNASTY: The Philadelphia/Baltimore Stars played in all three USFL Championship Games, winning in 1984 and 1985.

NOT SURE WHAT HE DID WITH IT, EXACTLY: Running back Kelvin Bryant of the Baltimore Stars (and later of the Washington Redskins) was the last player to touch the ball during a USFL game.

AND NO, WE'RE NOT PUTTING "PROFESSIONAL" IN SCARE QUOTES: The first professional football game ever broadcast on

ESPN was the 1983 USFL Season Opener featuring the Birmingham Stallions and the Michigan Panthers.

ON THE WHOLE, THEY WERE AVERAGE: The Washington Federals played two seasons in the USFL and had the worst record in the league each time. During both of those years, the Washington Redskins made it to the Super Bowl.

MR. TRUMP WAS NOT GOING TO BE UPSTAGED: Before the USFL folded, fans almost got a chance to see a "dream team" with leading passer Jim Kelly and leading rusher Hershel Walker as the Houston Gamblers and New Jersey Generals were considering a merger.

DID JFK HAVE MONEY ON THE PACK? Packers RB Paul Hornung was an active member of the U.S. Army during 1961 and had to get weekend passes in order to play football, including one approved by President Kennedy for the NFL Championship game.

THE FROZEN TUNDRA OF...WHAT? The original name of Green Bay's Lambeau Field was New City Stadium.

ONLY BECAUSE THE NORMALS CHANGED THEIR NAME: "Packers" is the oldest team nickname still in use in the NFL.

THE BLACK-AND-GREEN CREW: Packers Team founder Curly Lambeau had attended Notre Dame and thus adopted the colors blue and gold for his new team. Vince Lombardi changed the colors to the familiar green and gold in 1959. In the mid-1990s, GM Ron Wolfe considered changing the green back to blue but the idea fizzled.

NO, A STEEL CHAIR WAS NOT INVOLVED: Pro Wrestler Lex Luger spent some time on the Green Bay Packers injured reserve list in 1982.

PANNING FOR A COACH: The USFL's Denver Gold played for three seasons but had four head coaches.

ADMIRALS CAN STILL GET PROMOTED: Two Super Bowl starting quarterbacks (Kurt Warner and Jake Delhomme) were once members of the World League's Amsterdam Admirals.

IT'S BEEN A WHILE FOR CLEVELAND, BUT: The Cleveland Browns won the Championship of the AAFC all four years of its existence.

SO YOU MEAN SEATTLE DIDN'T MAKE UP THE WORD? There was once a team called the Miami Seahawks in the AAFC.

TOUGH ACTS TO FOLLOW: The first coach in Cowboys history to not win a Super Bowl was Chan Gailey, who was fired in 1999.

WE'RE NOT GOING TO LET A MAJOR AMERICAN TRAGEDY GET IN THE WAY OF BEER SALES: The Sunday following the assassination of President John F. Kennedy, the NFL played their games while the AFL voted to cancel theirs.

YEAH, IT'S EASIER WHEN YOU'VE GOT STEVE YOUNG AND JERRY RICE: George Seifert lost 32 games in 3 seasons as the Carolina Panthers' head coach.. He had only lost 30 in eight seasons as the San Francisco 49ers' head coach.

THIS IS WHY YOU NEED A MARKETING DEPARTMENT: Because of World War II, the Chicago Cardinals and the Pittsburgh Steelers combined in 1944 to form a team called Card-Pitt.

SOMEBODY ACTUALLY DID THE MATH: The Georgia Dome, home of the Atlanta Falcons, contains enough concrete to build a sidewalk from Atlanta to Cincinnati.

PLUS, YOUR FRIED EGGS WILL SLIDE RIGHT OFF: The Georgia Dome's Teflon roof only weighs 68 pounds.

THIS WASN'T A PROBLEM IN 1990: Traffic is such a problem at New England's Gillette Stadium that remote parking lots far from the stadium are more expensive to park in than lots closer to the stadium as they enable people to more easily get on the main highway.

CHEAP BEER, CHEAP VENUE: The Patriots old home, Foxboro Stadium (then known as Schaefer Stadium, due to a naming rights agreement with the brewery) was built in 1971 for $7.1 million – about $100 per seat. Its replacement, Gillette Stadium, cost $325 million to build in 2002.

BUT WHERE WERE THE LUXURY BOXES? The old home of the New Orleans Saints, Tulane Stadium, was the world's largest double-deck stadium when it opened in 1967.

ROAD WARRIORS: In 2005, the New Orleans Saints played "home" games in Giants Stadium, LSU's Tiger Stadium in Baton Rouge, and San Antonio's Alamodome thanks to damage done to the Superdome by Hurricane Katrina. The team went 1-7 at "home" and 3-13 overall.

FINALLY, SOME CHAMPIONSHIP-LEVEL FOOTBALL IN PONTIAC: The first indoor World Cup soccer match was played in 1994 at the Pontiac Silverdome, then-home of the Detroit Lions. Real grass was brought in for four games during the tournament, as artificial turf was not allowed.

TOO BAD THERE WAS NO GENIE INVOLVED: The Pontiac Silverdome used a series of air jets to float the one-piece artificial turf field over the stadium floor, a system called the "magic carpet".

EH, JUST PUT 'EM ANYWHERE THEY'LL FIT: When the Detroit Lions played at Tiger Stadium, both the home and visitor team benches were on the same side of the field.

BECAUSE IT NEVER REALLY RAINS HERE: In 2005, a roof was proposed for Kansas City's Arrowhead Stadium but voters defeated a ballot initiative to fund it.

TRUST ME GUYS, THIS IS JUST TEMPORARY: The first home of the Chargers in San Diego was Balboa Stadium...built in 1914 for a high school. The Chargers played there from 1961-1966.

TRY NOT TO TRIP OVER THE RUBBER: The first stadium that the Green Bay Packers called home was not Lambeau Field but rather Bellevue Park, originally built for minor league baseball.

A (COSTLY) MISTAKE BY THE LAKE: Cleveland Municipal Stadium, longtime home of the Browns, cost more to tear down in 1996 ($2.9 million) than it cost to build in 1931 ($2.5 million).

"JOINING THE BEAR CLUB" JUST DIDN'T HAVE THE SAME RING TO IT: Denver's old Mile High Stadium was originally named "Bears Stadium" and was meant for minor league baseball.

BUT NOT AT THE SAME TIME: Tampa Stadium (aka "The Big Sombrero") was the only stadium to host both a Super Bowl and a USFL Championship Game.

MAKE THAT TWO OLYMPICS: The former home of the Los Angeles Rams and Raiders, the L.A. Coliseum, is the only venue in the world to host an Olympics, a Super Bowl, and a World Series.

FREEZER BOWL WAS AN UNDERSTATEMENT: The wind chill factor during the 1982 AFC Championship Game between San Diego and Cincinnati was measured at minus 37 degrees Fahrenheit.

NOT MUCH TO DO IN THE WINDY CITY BACK THEN: Over 120,000 people once attended a high school game at Chicago's Soldier Field in the 1940s, a record that still stands.

STRUGGLING ARTIST: Steven Wright, the designer behind the Buffalo Bills helmet logo, had also designed a logo for the New England Patriots for use starting in 1980. However, the team owner put the old logo up against the new one for a vote during halftime of a game and the fans booed the new logo and thus it was never used. He also designed the infamous 49ers logo that was introduced but later mothballed due to fan outrage. Wright also designed prototypes for new Vikings and Chiefs logos that never made it on the field either.

DO NOT ADJUST YOUR TV SETS: In 1976, the Dallas Cowboys changed one of the blue stripes on their helmets to red to commemorate the nation's bicentennial.

IN OTHER WORDS, THEY WERE HANKERCHEFS: Before 1965, penalty flags used in the NFL were white.

NOT TO BE CONFUSED WITH A HYPOCYCLOID: The geometric shape of a football is a called a prolate spheroid.

YES, BALTIMORE WAS ONCE PART OF CANADA, THANK YOU VERY MUCH: The city of Baltimore has hosted champions of the NFL, CFL, and USFL.

MAYBE SOMEDAY: The city of Birmingham, Alabama has been the home teams in the WFL, USFL, WLAF, CFL, and XFL but never the NFL.

ADJUST YOUR SCORECARDS: Until 1909, a field goal was worth four points. Until 1912, a touchdown was worth five points

EH, WE'LL COUNT IT: The first victory for an AFL team over an NFL team was a preseason game when the Broncos defeated the Lions in August of 1967.

CALL IT PERMANENT VACATION: The Pittsburgh Steelers have no retired numbers, but by "coincidence" no Steelers have worn the numbers 12, 31, 32, 47, 52, 58, 59, 70, or 75 in recent years.

BUT THEN THEY WOULD HAVE BUILT THAT DOME FOR NOTHING: When Baltimore Colts owner Robert Irsay was looking for a new city for his team in 1983, he also considered Phoenix before deciding on Indianapolis.

LET'S GET IT RIGHT THIS TIME, FELLAS: The first win in the history of the Dallas Cowboys came on the opening game of their second season.

DON'T WORRY, GENTLEMEN, SOMEDAY WE'LL PLAY UNDER A GIANT BALLON: The Minnesota Vikings spent their beginning years playing in a stadium originally built for the AA baseball Minneapolis Millers.

THERE WERE PROBABLY MORE, BUT WE CAN'T PRINT THEM: The artificial turf at Philadelphia's Veterans was so bad it earned the nickname "Field of Seams'.

AND YOU THOUGHT VETERANS STADIUM HAD HARD TURF: The Buffalo Bills once played in War Memorial Stadium, a venue that also hosted stock car races in the early days of NASCAR.

THIS IS THE LAST TIME WE GET AN INTERN TO DO IT: In 2001, a preseason game between the Eagles and Ravens was cancelled because of a trench on the field – the artificial turf was not properly installed around the baseball sliding pits.

CHAPTER IV: FIRST HALF, BEER COMMERCIALS

IF FOUND GUILTY, THEY WERE SENTENCED TO HAVING WATCH MORE EAGLES GAMES: The behavior of Eagles fans during a Monday Night Football loss to the San Francisco 49ers in 1997 and a 34-0 loss to Dallas a year later was so bad that the City of Philadelphia assigned a Municipal Court Judge, Seamus McCaffrey, to the stadium on game days to deal with fans removed from the stands in what was referred to as "Eagles Court".

SNYDER'S LIST: As of 2013, the Redskins have a waiting list of over 160,000 people for season tickets.

MEET THE NEW BOSS, DIFFERENT FROM THE OLD BOSS: When the Redskin's Jack Kent Cooke Stadium (now known as FedEx Field), the site of the stadium was named Raljon after Cooke's sons' first names, Ralph and John. This ended when Daniel Snyder bought the team and the stadium's address is now officially in Landover, MD.

THANKS BUT NO THANKS. REALLY: Ashley Madison, an online dating site marketed to help people "cheat" on their significant others, unsuccessfully attempted to win naming rights to the new Giants/Jets stadium in 2010.

AND THEN THEY DECIDED TO TEAR IT DOWN: On September 14, 2003, the 366th regular season NFL game was played at Giants

Stadium, breaking a 50 year-old record held by Chicago's Wrigley Field.

WE PUT BUTTS IN SEATS: Only four NFL teams (the Redskins, Packers, Steelers, and Broncos) have never had a home game blacked out on local TV since the current blackout rules were put into place in 1973.

THE FROZEN TUNDRA OF (YOUR COMPANY HERE): Naming rights for Green Bay's Lambeau field are for sale, but as of 2013 no buyers have been found willing to accept the $100 million price tag.

JERRY SAYS YOU DON'T HAVE TO GO HOME BUT YOU CAN'T STAY HERE: In order to build the Cowboy's AT&T stadium, over 150 residences and small business buildings had to be demolished.

THE TRIANGLE PLAYER IS STILL A LITTLE JEALOUS: Trumpeter Tony DiPardo, leader of the TD Pack Band that played at every Kansas City Chiefs home game from 1960 to 2008, was awarded a Super Bowl ring for the Chief's victory in Super Bowl IV.

CAN'T BLAME THIS ONE ON THE ECONOMY: In 1961, the Denver Broncos drew fewer fans in the entire season than they do in a single home game today.

I GUESS THEY'D NEVER HEARD OF WHEELS: The retractable stands at Denver's Mile High Stadium were moved by pumping water into water bearings spaced out beneath them, lifting the structure off its foundation where hydraulic rams were able to push the stands forward or backwards.

IDENTITY CRISIS: As of 2013, Sun Life Stadium in Miami has been known as Joe Robbie Stadium, Pro Player Park, Pro Player

Stadium, Dolphins Stadium, Dolphin Stadium, and Land Shark Stadium.

SO INSTEAD OF UNBEARABLE, JUST MISERABLE: All Miami Dolphins home games during the month of September start at 4 PM due to the blazing Florida heat.

AND IT STILL HURTS TO BE TACKLED ON DIRT: While it used to be commonplace, as of 2014 only Oakland's O.co Coliseum currently hosts both an NFL and Major League baseball team.

UNTIL THAT TRAGIC TUNA-FISHING ACCIDENT: From 1966 to 1968 and later in the 1970s a live Dolphin was situated in a water tank in the open end of the Miami Orange Bowl.

GONE, BUT NOT ENTIRELY FORGOTTEN: Three venues that have hosted a Super Bowl are no longer standing: the Miami Orange Bowl, Tampa Stadium, and Tulane Stadium in New Orleans.

YOU HAD YOUR CHANCE: The Superdome attempted to lure the Oakland A's and Pittsburgh Pirates to New Orleans in the late 70s and early 80s. Due to reconfiguration of the lower seating bowl in 2011, the Superdome can no longer fit a baseball field within its confines.

HE HAD A POINT: David Dixon, the sports visionary who helped found the USFL, originally conceived of the idea for the Superdome, believing that the NFL would not reward a Super Bowl there without a new venue.

ONE OF MANY THINGS NOT QUITE RIGHT ABOUT THIS FILM: Baltimore's M&T Bank Stadium served as home field for the fictional Washington Sentinels in the 2000 Keanu Reeves film *The Replacements*.

LIKE A WRESTLING RING, ONLY LARGER: San Diego's Qualcomm Stadium was designed in the 1960s in the architectural style known as "Brutalism" with the shape being an "octorad" or "square circle".

HEY, IF THE GIANTS CAN PLAY IN JERSEY: The Oakland Raiders played their 1961 home season at San Francisco's Candlestick Park.

A TITANIC ADVANTAGE: The Tennessee Titans won their first 16 games at the stadium currently known as LP Field.

SOME THINGS EVEN PHILLY FANS WON'T PUT UP WITH: For the inaugural season at Lincoln Financial Field in 2003, the Eagles decided to ban hoagies and cheesesteak sandwiches being brought into the stadium. The ban lasted one week after being mocked by fans and radio hosts.

THIS WAS BEFORE "BREAST CANCER AWARENESS MONTH": In 2006, around 50,000 seats at Tampa's Raymond James stadium had to be replaced under warranty – they had faded from vibrant red to washed-out pink.

THE ULTIMATE TEST OF CEREBRAL FITNESS: The Bengals' Paul Brown Stadium hosts an annual chess tournament.

YEAH, BUT YOU SHOULD HAVE SEEN THE OTHER GUYS: The 2010 Seahawks were the first NFL team to ever win a division title with a losing record (in a season not shortened by a players' strike).

ACTUALLY, THE STADIUM ITSELF IS TOTALLY SILENT: The Seahawks' CenturyLink Field is listed in the Guniness Book of World records as the loudest stadium in the world.

TALK ABOUT STARTING OFF IN A HOLE: The quickest score in NFL history occurred on September 8, 2013 when the Steelers scored a safety three seconds into a game against the Titans. Titans returner Darius Reynaud fielded the opening kickoff in the field of play, stepped back into the end zone, and took a knee.

THIS WAS BEFORE THE ROOF CAVED IN: The Metrodome in Minneapolis is the only venue to host an MLB All-Star Game, a Super Bowl, an NCAA Final Four, and a World Series.

AND GAS WAS JUST TEN CENTS A GALLON: When the Cardinals hosted a playoff game on Jan 3, 2009, it was the teams' first home postseason game since the 1940s.

SO DON'T ASK THE TOUR GUIDE, IT WILL ONLY ANNOY HIM: Because at one time Chicago's Soldier Field could have its seating capacity modified from 74,380 to over 100,000 spectators, it's impossible to know for sure what was the largest crowd in the stadium's history. After a 2003 renovation the venue currently seats 61,500.

YOU GOTTA LET IT SETTLE FOR 50 YEARS OR SO BEFIORE YOU MOVE IN: Even though Soldier Field opened in 1924, the Bears did not make it their home until 1971 when they moved there from Wrigley Field, home of the Cubs.

SO LONG, FRIENDLY CONFINES: The 50 seasons the Bears spent at Wrigley Field was an NFL record until the Packers 51st season at Lambeau Field in 2007.

JUST MAKE IT FIT, OKAY? When the Bears played at Wrigley Field, the corner of the south end zone was cut off by the visitors' baseball dugout.

BUREAUCRATS RUIN EVERYTHING: When the NFL and AFL merged in 1970, the league passed a rule that each stadium must hold at least 50,000 fans. Wrigley Field only seated 47,000 for football which forced the Bears' move to Soldier Field.

BUREAUCRATS RUIN EVERYTHING PART 2: The Oakland Raiders explored moving home games to UC Berkley's Memorial Stadium in the early 70's and actually played one regular season game there in 1973 – a 12-7 victory over Miami. The City of Berkley passed a 10% tax on the gate receipts of pro sporting events, however, ending the possibility of a permanent move there.

NOTHIHNG LEFT TO ACCOMPLISH: On October 5, 2009, Brett Favre of the Vikings defeated his former team, the Packers, 30-23. This made Favre the first quarterback in NFL history to defeat each of the league's 32 franchises.

QUITE A SPREAD: The most lopsided betting line in NFL history was for a game on October 13, 2013: Jacksonville + 28 against Denver. The Broncos won (but failed to cover) 35-19.

NOT THAT IT WAS MISSED: There was no Pro Bowl (or other NFL all-star game) between 1943 and 1951.

LET'S MAKE THINGS INTERESTING: Intentional grounding is legal during the Pro Bowl.

FOR THOSE KEEPING SCORE AT HOME: During the 2008 Pro Bowl, four Redskins players (offensive tackle Chris Samuels, tight end Chris Cooley, and safety Ethan Albright) were all allowed to wear #21 in memory of their teammate Sean Taylor who had been murdered during the 2007 season.

WE DEMAND A REMATCH: The first NFL All-Star game was held in 1938 in Los Angeles. The New York Giants defeated the Pro All-Stars 13-10.

HOW MANY FREQUENT FLYER MILES DOES THIS GET YOU? Beginning with his rookie season, defensive lineman Merlin Olsen of the Rams played in 14 consecutive Pro Bowls.

I HOPE THEY MADE THE MOST OF IT: Despite being elected to the Hall of Fame, running back John Riggins and linebacker Ray Nitschke each only played in the Pro Bowl once.

YEAH, BUT DID HE GET TWO PAYCHECKS? In 2010, DeSean Jackson of the Eagles became the first player to be named to the Pro Bowl at two different positions: wide receiver and kick returner.

THIS EXPLAINS QUITE A BIT ABOUT HOW THE LEAGUE MAKES DECISIONS: NFL team owners could not agree on NFC conference alignment for the 1970 season, the first after the NFAFL merger. Five divisional alignment plans were suggested, and one was picked at random by Commissioner Pete Rozelle's secretary. (This is how Atlanta and New Orleans ended up the NFC West for many years.)

COINCIDENCE THEORY: The Buffalo Bills were named after the male Bison, or "Billy". Despite the similarity to the name of famous Wild West showman Buffalo Bill Cody, the team has never used "wild west" or "gunslinger" iconography.

DON'T CALL IT TEAL: The official name of the color used by the Carolina Panthers is "Process Blue".

DON'T GET ANY IDEAS: Under NFL rules, an NFL owner and his or her family only need to own 30% of the franchise to be considered the team's controlling owner.

AND YOU SHOULD SEE THE LITTER BOX: The six bronze panther statues that sit outside of the entrances at Bank of America Stadium in Charlotte are the largest sculptures ever commissioned in the United States.

AND THIS HAS WHAT TO DO WITH THE GRASSY KNOLL? According to former Bengals coach Sam Wyche, the NFL attempted to ban his no-huddle offense before the 1988 AFC Championship Game against the Bills. The league changed its mind after Wyche threatened to go public with the threat if the Bengals lost the game. (They ended up winning.)

WE DON'T REMEMBER THIS, EITHER: The original team colors of the Buffalo Bills were royal blue and silver.

WE MAKE IT LOOK EASY: The Miami Dolphins went from expansion team to Super Bowl champions in six years (1966-1972).

CHAPTER V: HALFTIME, CAR COMMERCIALS

OF COURSE: When the USFL filed an antitrust suit against the NFL, every NFL owner was named as a defendant except the Raider's Al Davis, who was a key witness for the USFL.

EITHER WAY, HE'S NOT GONNA WIN A SUPER BOWL: The first player picked in a USFL draft was the University of Pittsburgh's Dan Marino, who opted to join the NFL's Dolphins instead.

BRAIN TRUST: The USFL featured three future hall of fame coaches: Marv Levy, George Allen, and Sid Gillman.

MURDERER'S ROW: A total of 187 players spent time on both NFL and USFL rosters.

CHECK THE FORECAST: The USFL's Oklahoma Outlaws went 6-12 in their one season. All six victories were either in rain or snowstorms while all twelve losses were in domes or clear weather.

WE SHOULD HAVE KEPT THOSE GUYS AROUND: In the early 1950's, the Cleveland Browns drafted two players who would go on to become Hall of Fame coaches – Don Shula in 1951 and Chuck Noll in 1953.

AND WE USE THE TERM 'INSPIRED" LOOSELY: The Brown's orange and brown color scheme was inspired by the colors of Bowling Green University.

THIRD CHOICE: "HATED, BY THOSE GUYS": Rod Smart, who made the nickname "He Hate Me" famous as a member of the XFL's Las Vegas Outlaws, originally wanted "They Hate Me" on the back of his jersey but didn't have enough room.

WE CAN'T FIT THAT ON A HAT: The NFL was known as the American Professional Football Association from its founding in 1920 until 1922.

AT LEAST HE CAN BE PROUD OF ONE THING: Rashaan Salaam of the Memphis Maniax was the only Heisman Trophy winner to play in the XFL.

DUE TO BUDGET CONSTRAINTS, WE HAVE DROPPED THE "S": The Houston Texans of the WFL actually moved to Shreveport midway through the 1974 season. They were renamed the Steamer.

YEAH, YOU PROBABLY SHOULD LINE UP A STADIUM FIRST: The Detroit Wheels of the WFL folded during their first season, in part because they were unable to work out a deal to play at Tiger Stadium so their home games were 37 miles away at Eastern Michigan University in Yipsilanti.

WE HATE REDUNDANCY: The WFL had a team simply known as The Hawaiians. Calvin Hill, the Dallas Cowboys running back, was part of the team in 1975.

THINGS HAPPENED QUICKLY IN THE WORLD FOOTBALL LEAGUE: The New York Stars moved to Charlotte during their first season and were known as the Charlotte Stars for one game before renaming themselves the Hornets.

THE BELL ARE RINGERS: The WFL's Charlotte Hornets qualified for the 1974 playoffs but could not afford to travel. The Philadelphia Bell took their place.

NEVER SAY THEY WERE LACKING DIRECTION: The Memphis Southmen of the WFL were originally going to play in Toronto and be known as the Northmen but the Canadian government banned any pro football team that would compete with the CFL.

AND HE POURS A MEAN BEER: Philadelphia bartender Vince Papale (the subject of the film *Invincible*) played two years for the WFL's Philadelphia Bell before his stint with the Eagles.

AND THEY STILL HAVEN'T WON A SUPER BOWL: The Canadian Football League's Toronto Argonauts, founded in 1873, are the oldest professional football team in North America.

I'M NOT GOING TO BE HOME FOR DINNER: The Frankfurt Galaxy of the WLAF once had to travel over 5600 miles to play a "road" game against the Sacramento Surge.

OUT OF THE GATE, QUICKLY: In the 1967 NFL Championship Game, the Green Bay Packers scored 14 points in 12 seconds before the Dallas Cowboys offense had a chance to take the field. The Packers held off a Dallas comeback to win 34-27.

LET'S AIR SOME GREIVANCES: The classic 1982 AFC playoff game between San Diego and Miami was the first in NFL history to feature two quarterbacks (Dan Founts and Don Strock) passing for over 400 yards each. The Chargers won in overtime 41-38.

DON'T TAKE STOCK TIPS FROM THIS GUY: When the Cleveland Rams moved to Los Angeles after the 1946 season, they became the first team in a major professional sports league to call the West Coast home. Owner Dan Reeves had envisioned owning a team in Los Angeles for years, saying "it is going to be the greatest professional town in the country". Decades later, the Rams moved to St. Louis and Los Angeles has been without an NFL team since 1995.

BUT YOU KNOW PEOPLE STILL COMPLAINED: Tickets to what is now called Super Bowl I were priced between $6 and $12. The most expensive tickets for Super Bowl XLVIII in New York went for $2,600.

NOTHING GETS PAST THIS GUY: Before beginning the famous game-winning drive against the Bengals in Super Bowl XXIII, Joe Montana of the 49ers noticed comedian John Candy in the stands and pointed him out to a teammate. He went on to complete eight out of nine passes for 97 yards and a touchdown.

PAUL BROWN DOESN'T FORGET: In 1950, the Cleveland Browns defeated the defending champion Eagles 35-10 in the season opener, after which Philadelphia coach Greasy Neal called the Browns "a basketball team that can only pass". When the teams met again in December, the Browns again won, this time 13-7. They did not attempt a single pass.

FUN'S OVER, GUYS: Immediately after a 1941 game at New York's Polo Grounds between the Giants and the Brooklyn Dodgers, the stadium's public address announcer asks for all military personnel to report to their stations. The reason was the attack on Pearl Harbor earlier in the day.

WE'VE MADE A FEW ADJUSTMENTS: While many fans have heard of the 73-0 defeat of the Redskins by the Bears in the 1940 NFL title game, few are aware that the teams had met three weeks prior, with Washington winning 7-3.

YEAH, BUT WHO DID THE ACCOUNTING? In 1923, George Halas of the Chicago Bears set an NFL record that would last for 49 years when he returned a fumble 98 yards for a touchdown against the Oorang Indians. Halas was also the owner and coach of the Bears at the time. The player who fumbled was the legendary Jim Thorpe.

THIS IS REALLY IMPRESSIVE: The Houston Oilers' Earl Campbell in 1980 set a record by recording four 200-yard rushing games in a season. No other back in the league would run for 200 yards in a game that season.

THE FINAL COLOR BARRIERS: When the Oakland Raiders named Art Shell the first African-American head coach in NFL history in 1989, it was exactly 15 years to the day that Frank Robinson had become baseball's first African-American manager.

TOUGH BOSS: After a 17-7 loss to the Chicago Cardinals, Green Bay coach and GM Curly Lambeau was so upset with his teams' effort that he fined the entire team a half-game's pay. Lambeau told the media that the team "owes an apology to the people who paid good money to see it".

GENERAL MISCONCEPTION: Future NFL Hall of Fame quarterback Jim Kelly was pictured on the July 21, 1986 cover of Sports Illustrated as a member of the New Jersey Generals, who had acquired Kelly when the Houston Gamblers folded. Kelly never played a game for the Generals as the USFL ceased operations before the 1986 season began.

SHOWDOWN: Jerry Argovitz, owner of the USFL's Houston Gamblers, claims to have once challenged the Houston Oilers' owner Bud Adams to a game between their two teams in which the losing owner would pay $1 million to a charity of the winner's choice. (The game never happened).

BUT THE CARPET WAS REALLY NICE: The USFL's San Antonio Gunslingers were so cash-strapped the team's offices were in a double-wide trailer in the Alamo Stadium parking lot.

PROBABLY BEING USED FOR SPAGHETTI SOMEWHERE: The first trophy used by the NFL for its champion was the Brunswick-Balke Collender Cup, donated by the corporation of the same name. It was intended to be a traveling trophy like the Stanley Cup, and was awarded to the Akron Pros, champions of the inaugural 1920 season. The league then discontinued the trophy and its current whereabouts are unknown.

GONE, AND PRETTY MUCH FORGOTTEN: There are 53 defunct NFL franchises, mostly from the 1920s. The last franchise to fold was the Dallas Texans in 1952.

SORRY, NO WAY WE'RE LETTING IN A TEAM WITH *THAT* NAME: There existed a franchise in the AAFC named the Buffalo Bills who were denied entry into the NFL in 1950 when the leagues merged.

ONE TEAM TO UNITE US ALL: In 1940, a proposal was made to merge the Steelers and Eagles into a team that would be called the Pennsylvania Keystoners. The Keystoners were to play half their home games in Pittsburgh and half in Philadelphia. The league vetoed the plan.

PATRIOT GAMES: Former New England Patriots owner James Orthwein wanted to move the team to St. Louis in 1993. His effort was thwarted when Robert Kraft, who held the stadium lease, refused to let Orthwein out of the lease and eventually led a hostile takeover of the Patriots. Orthwein was a St. Louis native and it was rumored that the team would be renamed the Stallions. In 1995, the St. Louis Stallions were a proposed team for the expansion slot that was awarded to the Jacksonville Jaguars

DRAWING A BLANK: While the Cleveland Browns are famous for being the only NFL team not to use a helmet logo, during the mid-60's a proposal by the NFL was made to add a brown and white "CB" to the orange lids. The design appeared on some NFL promotional items but was never used in a game. Some speculate that it might have been used during the 1964 or 1965 preseasons.

THE FEW. THE PROUD: Of the 15 charter franchises of the NFL, only two survive today: the Chicago Cardinals (now known as the Arizona Cardinals) and the Dectur Staleys (now known as the Chicago Bears).

THEY ARE WHO WE THOUGHT THEY WERE: The Oorang Indians of 1922-23 were comprised entirely of American Indian players.

OKAY...IF YOU'RE GOING TO INSIST: While early NFL teams often featured black players, by 1934 the league was all white. It remained that way until 1945, when the Cleveland Browns moved to Los Angeles. A condition of being able to use the LA Coliseum was that the team be willing to integrate, so they signed two African-American players, Kenny Washington and Woody Strode.

BECAUSE THEY'RE RICH: During the summer of 1972, Carroll Rosenbloom and Robert Irsay, owners of the Baltimore Colts and Los Angeles Rams respectively, agreed to trade ownership of the two franchises with each teams' players and staff remaining intact.

NO, IT HAD NOTHING TO DO WITH MOBILE PHONES: The AFL's Los Angeles Chargers were named as such because the original team general manager liked the way the crowd at Dodgers and Southern Cal games would yell "charge" after a few notes from a bugle.

DON'T BOTHER RUNNING THIS BY LEGAL: The Cleveland/Los Angeles/St. Louis Rams were named as such because the original general manager's favorite college team had always been the Fordham Rams.

JUST DON'T ASK FOR GAME FOOTAGE: The first NFL game played under the lights took place on September 24th, 1930 when the Portsmouth Spartans defeated the Brooklyn Dodgers.

OR SO THEY CLAIM: The Washington Braves changed their nickname to the Redskins in 1933 upon the hiring of a Native American coach, Lone Star Dietz.

CHAPTER VI: SECOND HALF, FINANCIAL PLANNING COMMERCIALS

THIS TEAM WILL NEVER LOSE UNDER MY WATCH: The original owner of the Seattle Seahawks, Lloyd W. Nordstrom, died of a heart attack in January 1976, before his new team ever played a game.

A SOCCER GAME MUST HAVE BROKEN OUT: In 1934, nearly 80,000 fans at Chicago's soldier field watched the NFL champion Bears play a team of college all-stars to a scoreless tie in a game for charity.

BECAUSE HE'S DITKA: Legendary Chicago Bears coach Mike Ditka suffered a mid-season heart attack in 1990. He returned to the sidelines just ten days later.

YOU'RE GROUNDED: In 1998, Bears team President Michael McCaskey, the grandson of team founder George Halas, was fired . . . by his mother, Virginia.

RUNNING OUT OF GAS: The 1972 Falcons began their season by scoring 62 points in a win against the Saints. They lost their next three games, scoring a combined total of 15 points.

IT'S TIME: In 2002 the Cardinals moved from the NFC East to the NFC West, 15 years after relocating from St. Louis to Arizona.

UNORIGINAL SIN: In the early days of the NFL, it was not uncommon for football teams to "borrow" the nicknames of their city's baseball team. In addition to the New York Giants and St. Louis Cardinals, at one time or another the NFL featured teams named the New York Yankees, Brooklyn Dodgers, Cleveland Indians, Cincinnati Reds, Pittsburgh Pirates, Boston Braves, and Detroit Tigers.

AND THERE'S A HOFFA UNDER EACH ONE: The New York Giants have called six different stadiums home since 1935: The Polo Grounds, Yankee Stadium, the Yale Bowl, Shea Stadium, Giants Stadium, and MetLife Stadium.

CROWDED HOUSE: In 1975, New York's Shea Stadium was home to not only both the Giants and Jets, but also baseball's Mets and Yankees. The Yankees were having Yankee stadium renovated and the Giants were waiting completion of their new stadium in New Jersey.

PERFECTION COMES WITH A PRICE: After the first 0-16 season in NFL history, the Detroit Lions "rewarded" General Manager Matt MIllen with a $50 million buyout of his contract.

NO, THIS DOESN'T MEAN YOU GET FREE TICKETS: The Philadelphia Eagles nickname was chosen in 1933 to align with President Franklin D. Roosevelt's "New Deal" program. The National Recovery Administration used an eagle as its symbol.

GOOD THING IT WASN'T DONE ON TURKEY DAY: The NFL awarded a franchise to New Orleans on November 1st, 1966, which happened to be the date of All Saints Day. The ownership felt like it was a natural to call them the Saints.

THANKS FOR STICKING WITH US, FANS: In 1977, Tampa Bay did not score a touchdown at home until December 18, in the final game of the season.

CHAPTER VII: FINAL WHISTLE

A HARDY MELTDOWN: On opening day in 1950, Cardinals quarterback Jim Hardy threw eight interceptions. Hardy held the record for the most consecutive passes without an interception at the time (114).

AN INOFFENSIVE PERFORMANCE: On December 8, 2002, the expansion Houston Texans beat the Pittsburgh Steelers 24-6. What makes the game stand out is that the Texans amassed just 47 yards of total offense. Their three touchdowns came via interceptions and fumbles. No team has ever won a game with so few yards of offense.

A "SWEET" THROWING TOUCH: The greatest non-quarterback passer in modern NFL history is running back Walter Payton, who has thrown the most passes (34), thrown for the most passing yards (331), thrown the most touchdowns (8), and thrown the most interceptions (6).

STILL A NICE DEAL FOR THE GUYS WHO DON'T GET HIT: In the XFL, all players were paid $4,000 a game, except quarterbacks who received $5,000 and kickers/punters who got $3,500.

COMEDY DELAYS COMEDY: Saturday Night Live producer Lorne Michaels was infuriated when NBC's coverage of a double-overtime XFL game in February OF 2001 caused a highly anticipated episode of SNL to be delayed by 45 minutes.

MUCH LIKE McMAHON HIMSELF: Contrary to popular belief, the "X" in "XFL" did not stand for "extreme". According to founder Vince McMahon, it did not stand for anything.

AND THEY SAY IT'S NOT EXTREME: The XFL gave a postseason award to Shante Carver of the Memphis Maniax for "Hit of the Year" for a play where he knocked out Orlando Rage QB Jeff Brohm, a tackle which saw Brohm carted off the field and eventually rushed to the hospital.

THIS IS WHY THEY'RE STILL WEALTHY: Billionaires T. Boone Pickens and Mark Cuban originally committed to the UFL as team owners but both backed out prior to play beginning.

GOING OUT ON TOP: Two NFL teams won a league championship and then moved to a new city for the next season: the 1936 Boston Redskins (moved to Washington) and the 1945 Cleveland Rams (moved to Los Angeles).

I LIKE MY HAIR TO FLOW IN THE BREEZE: The last NFL player to play without a helmet was Dick Plasman, a lineman with the Bears, going bare-headed from 1937 to 1941, after which he joined the military to serve in World War II. When he returned, he played for three more seasons but wore a helmet as they became mandatory in 1943.

THE RATINGS CAN ONLY GET BETTER FROM HERE: The NFL's first televised game was on Oct 22, 1939 between the Brooklyn Dodgers and Philadelphia Eagles. It was broadcast by NBC to about 500 TV sets in New York and also to visitors to the World's Fair in New York.

YEAH, DON'T ASK: Only one basketball jersey is enshrined in the Pro Football Hall of Fame: a jersey worn by Hall of Fame member Mike Haynes (a cornerback with the Patriots and Raiders) during off-season charity events.

BECAUSE HE'S DEION: The Hall of Fame's collection of NFL memorabilia includes a black bandana worn by Deion Sanders. Sanders had tied the bandana to his bust during his enshrinement ceremony.

TRIPLE CROWN: Dan Reeves, Tony Dungy, and Mike Ditka have all appeared in Super Bowls as players, assistant coaches, and head coaches.

MASTER OF THE SECONDARY: Ronnie Lott of the 49ers and Raiders received All-Pro honors at three different positions – cornerback, free safety, and strong safety.

GREEN DAY: Quarterback Trent Green, of the Rams and Chiefs, once appeared on the TV game show *Wheel of Fortune*.

BUT DID HE AT LEAST GET A JERSEY TO HOLD UP? Michael Vick, quarterback for the Falcons and Eagles, was drafted by the Colorado Rockies despite not having played baseball since the 8th grade.

HE GOT THINGS COOKING: While a student at LSU, Indianapolis Colts running back Joseph Addai was a frequent guest on the Food Network's *Emeril Live* show.

HIS POLITICAL SWANN SONG: In 2006, Hall of Fame wide receiver Lynn Swann unsuccessfully ran for governor of Pennsylvania.

IT'S ALL DOWNHILL FROM HERE: When Colts Rookie Bert Rechichar lined up for his first NFL field goal attempt in 1953, he broke the record by kicking a 56-yarder.

IT WAS A DIFFERENT TIME: Hall of Fame quarterback Otto Graham and TV's "Rifleman" Chuck Connors both played for the 1945 Rochester Royals of the National Basketball League . . . and their team won the league championship.

SO THEY ENDED UP IN MISSOURI, HOW? During their final season in Chicago, the 1959 Cardinals played four home games at Soldier Field and two in Minnesota, in an attempt to find a new home.

A PEACH OF A DEAL: In 1964, a group from Georgia approached the St. Louis Cardinals ownership about moving the team to Atlanta, where a new stadium was being built. There was a new stadium under construction as well in St. Louis but it was behind schedule and the team was suffering financially. The St. Louis stadium authority eventually matched Atlanta's offer and the team stayed put.

IN OTHER WORDS, YOU HAD TO BE REALLY RICH: The only requirement for a team to join the original version of the NFL was to pay the entrance fee of $100.

NO, THEY WERE NOT PLAYING BASEBALL: The lowest scoring playoff game in NFL history was the 1970 NFC Wild Card Game where the Dallas Cowboys defeated the Detroit Lions by a score of 5-0.

BROWNOUT: The Cincinnati Bengals' first game in Paul Brown Stadium was against the Cleveland Browns, a team named after its founder Paul Brown, who was also the Bengals' founder.

THEY WILL COME, THEN YOU WILL BUILD IT: The Green Bay Packers were organized in the editorial room of the old Green Bay Press-Gazette building in 1919. Their first season, they went 10-1 against other teams from the area while playing in an open field with no fences or bleachers. Fans "passed the hat" for donations to help fund the team.

THE VERDICT IS IN: The Green Bay Packers almost came to an end in 1933 when a fan won a $5,000 verdict against the team after falling from the stands at City Stadium. This put the team's insurance company out of business, and the team was put into receivership. Local businessmen had to raise $15,000 to save the franchise from folding.

IT WAS EITHER THAT OR THE NEW YORK NOISE: The New York Titans' nickname change to the Jets in 1963 was inspired by their new stadium's location next to LaGuardia Airport.

ANYTHING TO KEEP PAYROLL LOW: The Jets' signing of quarterback Joe Namath for a then unheard of $427,000 in 1964 is generally credited with bringing together the NFL and AFL, as NFL owners wanted a common draft to prevent bidding wars for top players. In return, they agreed to play the AFL in a championship game now known as the Super Bowl. By 1966, the two leagues agreed to a merger that was effective for the 1970 season.

NEW YORK, NEW YORK: The first game between the New York Jets and New York Giants took place on November 1, 1970 at Shea Stadium. A sold-out crowd watched the Giants win 22-10.

TELL US HOW YOU REALLY FEEL: In October of 1983 the New York Jets called Shea Stadium "rundown, neglected and the NFL's poorest facility for athletes and spectators alike" while announcing that they were moving to New Jersey to share Giants Stadium with their NFC rivals.

USUALLY THIS WAS NOT A BIG DEAL: The Jets' lease at Shea Stadium required that they not play their first home game until the Mets' season was finished. In 1969, the defending Super Bowl champions didn't play a home game until October 20th thanks to the Mets' World Series run.

BUT THEN THEY WERE LIKE, "EH, WHO CARES?" In 2008, the NFL considered a rule that would ban hair long enough to cover a player's name on the back of his jersey.

STOP YANKING US AROUND: There were two professional football teams known as the New York Yankees (NFL, 1927-28, AAFC , 1946-49) and a third known as the New York Yanks (NFL, 1950-51).

THEY'LL NEVER NOTICE US IN THESE: In 2013 Seattle police started patrolling the stands during Seahawks games while undercover . . . wearing the visiting team's jerseys.

AND THOSE SCHOOLS WERE INSULTED: The expansion Tampa Bay Buccaneers originally chose orange and green instead of orange and red for their team colors. The reason they switched was because both the University of Miami and Florida A&M already used those colors.

NO LAUGHING MATTER: The infamous "Bucco Bruce" logo worn on the helmets of the early Buccaneers teams was designed by the local newspaper's cartoonist.

GO FIGURE, IT'S NIKE: For the 2011 Pro Bowl, Nike designed football pants that continued halfway down the player's shins instead of stopping right past the knee like traditional uniforms do.

Also from Jester-Daye Publishing:

The New Conspiracy Handbook:

From G.I. Joe to Lady Gaga...25 Truths You Won't Find on Wikipedia

by Simon Trinculo.

Ever wonder if things are not always as they seem? The New Conspiracy Handbook offers an opportunity to see a little of what goes on behind the curtain. This is your guide to 25 brand new theories that take you beyond the usual topics and will give you a new perspective on our culture and history.

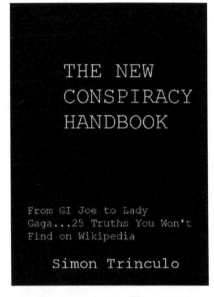

THE NEW CONSPIRACY HANDBOOK

From GI Joe to Lady Gaga...25 Truths You Won't Find on Wikipedia

Simon Trinculo

From music to sports, from science to politics, The New Conspiracy Handbook tackles a wide variety of topics. Find out what really happened to Osama Bin Laden; learn about the actor murdered to increase box office sales; discover which famous Founding Father has a mysterious past, filled with unexplained deaths and inexplicably rapid promotions.

Whether you are a conspiracy theory buff, a dogged skeptic, or just a casual reader looking for something thought-provoking, this is the book for you. When you read The New Conspiracy Handbook, expect to learn, to be entertained, and to think about a number of topics in a completely new light.

Do you dare open your eyes to the truth?

Made in the USA
Lexington, KY
16 July 2016